SUBIC

A SAILOR'S MEMOIR
Based on the Story of Bobby Earl Perkins

SUBIC
A SAILOR'S MEMOIR
Based on the Story of Bobby Earl Perkins

Barbara Perkins-Brown, Ed.D

Copyright © 2015 Barbara Perkins-Brown

Cover Design & Graphics:
Barbara Marie Perkins Sabillo

All Rights Reserved

ISBN-10: 0692483594
ISBN-13: 978-0692483596

No part of this publication may be reproduced or transmitted
in any form or by any means without obtaining
permission from the author or publisher.

PRINTED IN THE UNITED STATES OF AMERICA

In Memory of

Bill Cash, USN
Morris G. Ervin, USN
Donald Moore, USN
&
Those U.S. Servicemen Stationed in
Subic Bay Naval Base, Philippines
BOAT POOL 1967 - 1968

CONTENTS

Introduction

1	1967	1
2	THE CITY	9
3	THE BOAT	16
4	THE BROTHERHOOD	27
5	THE ACCUSED	43
6	THE TEAM	53
7	THE RANK	57
8	THE WOUND	64
9	THE MESS HALL	70
10	THE OUTCRY	77
	In Retrospect	85

References:

US Navy Rank	91
Military Time	93

Thank you DADDY for letting me write and share your story.

--Barbara--

INTRODUCTION

It is an engraved memory. My father could never forget the time he had spent in Subic Bay Naval Base, Philippines. Subic is truly unforgettable--a blend of great adventures and great adversaries. Subic is quite a paradise, and no one can completely walk away from it because its memory is enduring.

This memoir, in a parallel struggle for equality and human dignity, reflects the civil rights movements happening back on U.S. soil during the late 1960s. Also, this story is told in remembrance of my father's friends who served as the pillar of strength for him and for many back in the boat pool, and in honor of those fearless members of the Black Study Group who stood together against all odds to fight a battle for all the Blacks stationed in Subic. For my father, they were the unsung heroes who used the power of pen to persistently inform those in authority to recognize their outcry against the on-going oppressions in the military. *This is also their story.* The Black Study Group's monumental risk-taking effort had finally paid off--justice prevailed! These unsung heroes had made it possible for the next sailors, marines, and other servicemen who were stationed in Subic to have their constitutional rights protected. *This book is for them.* However, some names were intentionally changed to protect the identities of certain individuals.

History is also on the side of these sailors. Despite of being in a foreign land, they persevered so that the American ideals--life, liberty, and justice--would always be upheld to the highest standards regardless of one's skin color. Finally, my father shares this personal journey not to shame the U.S. Navy but to recount his struggles against discrimination and how his Christian faith had ushered him out of this plight. It is hoped that this book would bring light and inspiration to many.

                                      Barbara Perkins-Brown, Ed.D
                                      dr.barbarabrown@yahoo.com
                                      www.BarbaraPerkins-Brown.com

A SAILOR'S MEMOIR
Based on the Story of Bobby Earl Perkins

Bobby Earl Perkins

CHAPTER 1

1967

I was twenty-three years old, a sailor in the U.S. Navy. While on my military leave in Montgomery, Alabama, my hometown, I became ill and was eventually admitted to Maxwell Air Force Base Hospital. I was treated for abdominal pain, and after three days of thorough treatment, I was then released. Two days earlier, I was scheduled to be shipped off to Subic Bay Naval Base in the Philippines for my new assignment right after my last duty station with USS Orleck DD886, a naval warship out of Vietnam. Because of my sudden illness, the Navy Reserve Center in Montgomery had been informed about my medical condition, and the navy center sent a speed letter to Subic that I would be reporting two days late as ordered.

February 6, 1967. The day had come. Six extensive years had eventually gone by since I joined the U.S. Navy in 1961. I was only 17 then. Now, I finally arrived in Subic Bay. Wearing my Service Dress White uniform--a short-sleeved white button-up shirt with open collar, white trousers and a belt, a white cap, and white dress shoes--I reported to the personnel department for in-processing, and after a couple of hours of waiting patiently in the receiving room, I was told to proceed to the base master-at-arms, also known as the base police. From there, I was ordered to see the base captain to account for my late arrival.

The captain's office was on the second floor of the personnel building, and it did not take that long for me to find it. As I walked into a small office, I saw a White navy officer. He was Captain James A. Lewis, and his name was spelled out on an engraved-gold nameplate sitting on the middle of his desk. He was in his mid-fifties, red-faced, almost bald, and at that moment, he was looking through a couple of papers in his hands while sitting behind a wide-wooden desk. He looked sharp in his decorated military uniform, but he also appeared ill-tempered and somewhat arrogant in demeanor. Noticing my possibly unwanted presence, the captain stopped what he was doing and rose up from the chair. He was about six-feet tall.

"The navy will not put up with you people! Bucking the navy!" Slamming the papers on his desk, the captain opened in a harsh and loud voice and proceeded to reprimand me, "I will take that crow off your arm (to reduce in rank)! All of you-- young Black sailors ain't nothing but trouble makers, and your action is setting a derogatory nature to the other Blacks in here!" Wagging his finger at me, he continued, "And this won't be tolerated nor condoned aboard Subic Naval Base! Do you have anything to say?" At last, the captain concluded in his sudden anger but with obvious intimidation.

I had become very nervous. I could feel my words were somehow getting chocked in the corner of my dry throat. I did not know where to start to explain the circumstances of my delay. However, before I was able to utter a word, a legal navy officer in his dignified Service Dress Khaki uniform promptly marched in with a letter in his hand. The officer rendered a military salute and handed the envelope to the frowning captain, and then without any single word and with another salute to finalize his visit, the legal officer immediately exited the room. I already knew what the letter was. It was the speed letter sent by the Navy Reserve Center in Montgomery, Alabama, which detailed my recent illness and my subsequent delayed arrival to the Philippines.

    The base captain opened the letter and took some time to read its contents. There was no reaction on his face, but the frown remained visible on his wrinkled forehead. Meanwhile, I stood up there in silence waiting for at least a favorable reaction from the captain. I was hoping that the message would somehow enlighten him about the circumstances of my tardiness.

After reading the letter, the captain looked at me in a scrutinizing manner. I could tell he was not easy to please. I maintained my silence. I even kept my head down to avoid his piercing blue eyes.

"I hope you learn something here today," he reasoned calmly, but his spiteful attitude remained unchanged, and the tone of his voice was still harsh and hostile.

Sensing that I was not yet out of trouble, I replied in a low tone, "I did, sir!"

"You better keep your mouth shut when you find yourself in shit up to your nose!" He warned me, which made me feel more uneasy.

Next, the captain motioned with his two hands up in the air for me to get out of his office, as if I were a fly he was trying to shoo away. Without any sign of uncertainty, I left the office in haste, feeling like I was quite fortunate to escape a near death sentence--I thought to myself. It was a big relief! Then, I continued moving to the supply office to report for my duty assignment.

While I was on my way to the supply department, the beauty and vastness of the naval base did not escape my eyes. I was captivated and amazed! My first impression of Subic Bay was very pastoral and respite. Suddenly, a slight smile eventually appeared on my weary face, and at the same time, my curious eyes roved around, admiring the sceneries: the harbor, the water, the mountains, and the warm weather. I could tell that Subic had been blessed with rich natural resources.

After a long and tiresome journey, my heart was suddenly at ease despite the earlier encounter with the irate base captain. I was hoping that whatever I was about to experience here, it would be an adventure of a lifetime, and I was ready to make my stay a great one here in *Subic.*

CHAPTER 2
The City

The Subic Bay Naval Base was in the City of Olongapo, within the province of Zambales, which was a two-hour drive from Manila, the capital of the Philippines. Subic Bay, an inlet of the South China Sea, was in its strategic location as the largest naval facility in the Philippines. It played a very important role during the Vietnam War, especially with the U.S. involvement between the 1950s and 1960s.

During the Vietnam War, a tremendous workload was entrusted to Subic Bay. It was the service station for the U.S. Seventh Fleet, the largest armed force with 60-70 ships and 200-300 aircrafts that helped ensure security and stability around the Asia-Pacific region. The naval base served as support for the U.S. ships that sailed in the Pacific Oceans and South China Sea. Ships came to Subic for supplies, repairs, and rest and relaxation for the ship crew. The area was tropical, with a high temperature around 95 degrees and a low temperature of about 70 degrees during the rainy seasons.

The base had a big hospital, the U.S. Naval Hospital, located on top of a hill, also called Cubi Point. The base had 726 enlisted personnel, of which 74 were Black servicemen. This statistical information was displayed and regularly updated on the status board located at the personnel office, letting all base workers know how many people were on board, as well as job openings and statuses. The base also employed about 200 Filipino workers for civil service with no fringe benefits like retirement and medical coverage. Aside from sailors and seamen, U.S. Marine personnel were also performing security duties on base. Subic had several departments consisting of service craft, supply, food service, postal, administration, engineering, education, chaplain, naval investigative service, base command staff, area command staff, and admiral flag staff.

    The metropolis of Olongapo was outside the gate of Subic Bay Naval Station. The Kalaklan River, a drainage channel that spanned from the downtown area through the city's cemetery, separated the main streets from the base. Crossing over this river was a wide bridge known as the Kalaklan Bridge that connected the U.S. military gate to the city.

Olongapo, at that time, had a population of about 100 thousand people. The Filipinos, just like most Asians, were very hospitable and friendly to foreigners. The city's visitor's spot was divided into two sections. The major highway was Magsaysay Drive, and at the end of it, on the right, was Charles Town--this was the first section, where one would find bars, hotels, movies, restaurants, and mini-stores for the Whites. The other part of the city was on the left side of Magsaysay Drive leading to Rizal Avenue, also called "The Jungle," which was the area for the Blacks. Just like the Whites, the Blacks had their own designated locations for bars, hotels, restaurants, barbershops, tobacco and alcohol stores, and gift shops.

Around The Jungle area, on each side of the street was a long line of bars, both big and small, providing night-time entertainment, leisure, games (darts, cards, and pool tables), good times, and even party girls for servicemen. Many bars had security guards to keep females who were not their workers out, and only those females with a male escort could come in for a night of fun and good time.

Each bar had about 10-20 female employees working as hostesses or bargirls. These bargirls earned their money through commissions by getting customers to buy their drinks and by having a date with their patrons, who were required to pay a bar fine to the bar owner for their time out from work. Many sailors would come to these bars to hang out, relax, drink, and get a date after a day's work or on a weekend.

The city's public transportations were the tricycle cabs and jeepneys. The tricycles were motorcycles with a one-wheeled sidecar and could accommodate up to three passengers, two inside the sidecar and one on the back of the driver, and they cost less than a quarter per ride to any point within the city limit. These tricycles were good for short distance and on tight roads where a full-sized vehicle could not access. On the other hand, the jeepneys were much cheaper than the tricycles. Most of the time, these jeepneys were generally packed and crowded with 16 or more passengers even though they were not equipped with air-conditioning but only with wide-open windows. The jeepneys were remnants of the U.S. Army three-bucket military jeeps from World War II, which were redesigned by Filipinos making the jeep longer and adding a two-yard seat on each side in order to have the capacity of a mini-bus.

    Olongapo City had a so-called red light district where strip clubs and adult theaters were heavily concentrated, and many times this area would be off-limits to servicemen because of suspected drug-trafficking and prostitution. The city had a curfew from 0200 hours till 0600 hours, and all military personnel must be off the street. The main gate of the base, which was at the other end of the Kalaklan Bridge, would close down the same hours as the curfew. All streets off Magsaysay Drive were out of bound for military servicemen, unless one had an out-of-bound pass issued by the base personnel office in **Subic.**

CHAPTER 3

The Boat

It was quite a walk. I was very exhausted from carrying my gear and duffle bag from one place to the next. But I was able to enjoy my time and had the chance to get acquainted with my new environment, possibly my new home. When I arrived at the supply office, I was commanded to see the chief-in-charge at once. His name was Chief William Turner.

After learning the direction to the chief's office, I wasted no time to get there. When I finally reached his office, Chief Turner was standing by the door already waiting for me. The chief was a freckled-White man with choppy-brown hair in his early forties and stood about five-foot ten. During my meeting with Chief Turner, he informed me that there were two billets provided for the cooks. One was in the main mess hall, and the other was in the service craft.

"You will be assigned to Tug Boat 4TB774 and your chief's name is Chief Griffith. Get your gear and the truck will take you to your boat," ordered Chief Turner in his husky monotone voice. "All of your soul brothers are down at the service craft," he continued, "I think you'll feel right at home there."

The chief did not give me the opportunity to ask or say something, and after providing me brief information about my duty, he immediately sent me away.

Just like what I was told, I got my gear, got on the truck, and got to my assigned boat. The service craft division was about two miles away from the main part of the base. My immediate chain-of-command, Chief Thomas Griffith met me at Tug Boat 4TB774. He was a six-foot tall White man in his late thirties with a tan complexion and dirty blonde hair. He took me aboard to show me the different parts of the boat. Next, he showed me where I would sleep and where I would cook. I was going to be assigned at the galley, where all the food supply for the entire crew was kept and where everyone working on my boat would likely eat. To carry on my daily assignment, I would wear the prescribed uniform--an apron, a plain shirt, a pair of pants, and a chef hat--all in white. The navy trained me as a commissary supply, who was also knowledgeable in preparing meals for the military, and that was exactly what I was expecting to execute while on this post.

The entire support crew working at my boat consisted of six people, of which one was a Filipino young man in his early twenties. His name was Felipe, but he was commonly referred to as "Houseboy." His job was to keep the boat clean and to help in the galley. Houseboy was paid every two weeks by the crew; each crew member contributed $5.00 per payday as Houseboy's salary.

The mission of the tug boat I was assigned to was to help large ships dock at the pier known as the boat pool. In the boat pool area, there were ten crafts all together. These crafts were composed of two large tugs, four small tugs, two water boats, and two garbage barges. The tugs maneuvered vessels by pulling and pushing them on the water.

All ten crafts had one Black cook assigned on duty. Only the garbage barges had Black personnel in charge. Every day the garbage boats would come around the boat pool area to take all the trash and rubbish from the ten crafts and then dump these refuse out to the sea as far as three or four miles away.

Within a couple of days of my arrival, I had already befriended the other Black servicemen on base. It appeared to me that all the Blacks at the boat pool seemed to stick together to help each other out. First, I met two Black officers: Boatswain's Mate Michael Parker, in charge of the garbage barge; and Boatswain's Mate Norman Wilson, a shoreline security patrol who monitored the base harbor's territorial boundaries. They were both Petty Officers Second Class (PO2) in their late twenties and with more than ten years of naval service. A Boatswain's Mate (BM) was to supervise the ship's crew in maintaining the boat's structure and equipment.

On BM Wilson's boat, the cook was PO2 Bill Cash from Cleveland, Ohio with seventeen years of naval service. PO2 Cash was the senior cook in the entire boat pool, and most of the Black sailors and marines, especially the younger ones, looked up to him for leadership and guidance. He was like everyone's "Big Daddy." PO2 Cash had a slightly big belly and a brown-skin complexion. He was tall, bald, and in his early fifties.

On my boat, I cooked breakfast and lunch daily. I would also prepare sandwiches with fresh meat, as well as baked produce for the crew to eat at their pleasure. Most of the crew would leave the boat at about 1400 hours unless a large ship was coming to Subic, and if so, then all boats were on call.

Every Monday and Wednesday, all navy cooks from each ship would go to the boat pool's supply store with their written requisitions to order whatever they needed to prepare their meals, such as meat, canned goods, bread, milk, fruits, flour, sugar, and vegetables for the crew. The cook had a say on the meal plan and what to order for the galley.

At the supply store, I met a tall Black sailor from Louisiana in his mid-twenties, PO2 Ronald King, who worked at the store as a clerk. He and I became good friends, and once in a while, we would hang out together after work.

One mid-day, PO2 Cash came to my boat unexpectedly.

"How are you doing here so far, Perkins? And if you need anything or if you need help with something, just let me know," PO2 Cash offered.

"Everything is fine, sir," I replied with a smile but with a wondering face.

Then he asked me in a low tone but with heaviness in his voice, "How is Chief Griffith with you? Is he treating you okay? I guess you probably heard by now that he had a Black cook before you, and he dogged him out. He don't care for the Blacks, so beware of him!" PO2 Cash warned me with an obvious concern in his eyes.

Hoping to dispel his worries, I positively assured PO2 Cash, "Well, so far he hasn't said anything about my work, or if he wanted anything changed about the way I do my job."

A week later after that brief conversation with PO2 Cash, Chief Griffith questioned me while I was doing my usual routine at the galley--cooking and food inventory.

"What did PO2 Cash want on my boat, Perkins? Why was he here last week?"

"PO2 Cash was just trying to know if I needed any help since he is the senior cook at the boat pool and that I am new," I reasoned out unsuspectingly.

"Bull Shit!" Chief Griffith shouted in my face. "I know about the game you people play if you can't get your ways! If you need help, I am the chief of my boat and I don't need outside help from PO2 Cash or any other!"

I could immediately sense how condemnatory he was about PO2 Cash, and yet I tried to be agreeable to be on his good side.

"You're the chief, S-S-Sir, and I will do what's best for the boat and the crew."

"If you know what's good for you, you better keep the ship in shape!" Chief Griffith concluded as he walked away in thundering footsteps.

I remained standing still. And even though he was already gone, I could still feel the intensity of his anger; he sounded like a roaring lion ready to devour its helpless prey alive. I knew for sure that there was a serious threat revealed in the chief's sudden outrage. At this point, I felt like a one-legged man in a butt-kicking contest, where there was no chance of winning. Now, I began to see that aside from its hospitable environment, there was this oppressive side gradually unveiling itself in the face of *Subic.*

Subic: A Sailor's Memoir

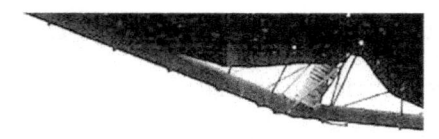

PO2 Bobby Perkins

Subic Bay, Philippines

1967

CHAPTER 4

The Brotherhood

For the next few days everything went well with me, with the people I worked with, and with the activities on the boat. Then after a couple of busy weeks, I finally got a chance to go to the Base Exchange to get some Personal items, such as toiletries, undergarments, and hair products.

While I was at the exchange, I had a hard time looking for Black hair products. I asked a young Filipino saleslady where to find Black hair care items.

"No, the base no order," she responded in her broken English accent as she continued to straighten the racks of magazines situated near the entrance door.

I did not know what else to think at that very moment except wondering what to do with my nappy hair, and I was truly disappointed to learn that Black sailors were sent to this naval facility, which was away from home, and that they were not well provided for. And then, when I was ready to pay for my items, the Filipino saleslady told me to wait until she finished assisting all the White customers regardless of who got there first. Later on, I learned from the other Black servicemen that the Filipino workers at the Navy Exchange were ordered by their superior to treat the "Niggers" differently. Every time a White man would come into the store, the longer I had to wait. And it was very obvious that the workers at the exchange treated the Whites better than the Blacks. I felt like I was back in Alabama and was experiencing racial segregation all over again. I just had to wait for my turn until a White customer had completed his shopping.

Meanwhile, as I was standing in line waiting to be checked out, I noticed that there were no copies of Black magazines on the racks--no *Jet*, *Tan*, *Ebony*, or any other Black publications. And that was not all! I remembered noticing the presence of a Chinese tailor who would come to the boat pool once a week for any servicemen wanting his service, and most Black sailors got their clothes tailor made simply because the base store did not carry Black wear, such as dashiki and bottom-up shirts in vibrant colors. Were you kidding me? No available merchandise for the Blacks! No hair-dressing products, no magazines, and no African inspired clothing! This was a scary reality. How could the U.S. Government allow "this" to happen to us? A simple question! But no one seemed to know the answer, or perhaps, if someone did know the answer, that person would probably never even bother to say a word.

February 1968. It had been almost a year since I got to Subic Bay. One morning, I informed Chief Griffith that I was going to take the navy-wide exam for the next pay grade. I was an E-4 (PO3) and hoping to get my rank promoted to E5 (PO2).

"Houseboy can do it as well as you! And you don't need PO2 Cash to come and take your place, do you?" Chief Griffith sarcastically commented.

The next morning, I woke up earlier than usual to get myself ready, and then I proceeded directly to the examination venue.

I was very confident and well prepared since I had been reading and studying diligently for the test, and on top of that, I had been praying earnestly. After taking the navy-wide exam, I returned to the boat to change from my military uniform to my civilian outfit. Next, I went to town for a haircut. I had to get out of the base for a haircut because there was nobody there who could cut Black folk's hair. When my haircut was done, I stopped by at one of the bars at The Jungle area. While I was inside the bar enjoying a cold bottle of beer and some soul music, I came across PO2 King, the clerk from the supply store. We had a pleasant conversation and a couple of drinks. Then, he mentioned about the Black Study Group.

"Have you met any of the brothers at the Post Office?" PO2 King asked.

I took a sip first, and then I gave him a puzzling look and shook my head.

He continued, "They have this Black Study Group every Monday at 1900 hours in Building P. Why don't you stop by to meet the brothers?"

"Sure, I will check it out" I affirmed.

The next Monday, I decided to go to Building P. It was quite a meeting. I came in and met the rest of the Black sailors and marines stationed in Subic. I was curious, so I stayed in for the entire meeting and learned that the Black Study Group did not only aim to focus on the history and culture of the Black people, but the group's existence was also significantly fundamental in maintaining the dignity of the Black servicemen. The group served as an overseer in preventing the escalation of possible violence in the naval facility due to racial tension.

The meeting would usually start with PO2 James Barks, a slim preacher from Charlotte, South Carolina and a Chaplain's volunteer, who would say a passionate prayer and would read aloud a couple of Bible verses that were somehow relevant to the plights of the Blacks in Subic. Then the group would discuss and analyze any mistreatments or injustices that had happened to each of them lately and what they could possibly do about these aggravated incidents of discrimination.

Next, the group would start gathering everyone's testimony and suggestions, which would be recorded in a log book. Finally, they would review the correspondence that had been progressively in the making; they would add new information or details to the already lengthy letter. The drafted letter would be sent outside the naval command as the Black Study Group's final step to combat racism. It was decided that someone outside Subic had to know what was going on over here so that our constitutional rights could be protected. These were some of the views expressed in the letter:

"The authorities who are supposed to carry out these laws are doing it not according to the UCMJ (Uniform Code of Military Justice)... We are asking that an investigation from outside officials of the laws be held... We are not plotting or accusing anyone of anything... We see plainly that these laws are used to relegate us into bad positions and keep us there. We as Black Americans are subjected to racism and it is hidden through so called legal action."

Also the following instances were some of the injustices highlighted in the letter:

The captain presiding over the charges against a naval member adjusted the laws based on who was being tried; the captain swore the Oath of the USN, but because of his obvious racist attitude, he violated his own oath blatantly. Another issue was about a Petty Officer with 16 years of service who had broken his arm one day and worn a cast on

> We want justice. We are seeking what is rightfully ours.
>
> The harsh penalties, the unjustified incidents, that can't be explained
> total
> We the under signed; make up only a small percentage, of the total percentage of the black american Sailors and Marines. We sign below, because this is a clear call for Justice. We ask the higher official and the white enlisted personnel to recognize the dignity of the Black American Serviceman.

A partial copy of the drafted letter signed by the members of the Black Study Group stationed in Subic Bay Naval Base, Philippines his arm from his wrist to his shoulder for almost a month; however, due to his medical condition that limited his job performance, his quarterly marks were dropped very low keeping him from getting the advanced rate he was fully qualified for. Then another instance was with a Black seaman who was charged with assault and battery for fighting a White sailor who called him "Nigger." The Black seaman was told that under the U.S. Constitution, the White man had all the rights to speak his mind.

    Later on that night, I was introduced to one of the group's speakers, PO2 Morris G. Ervin, a postal clerk in his mid-twenties. He and I immediately became good friends, and from then on, he was my "homeboy." I was grateful to find out that PO2 Ervin was also from the South--Alabama. His hometown was Birmingham, which was about an hour away from Montgomery, where I was from.

PO2 Ervin had big Afro hair and wore a pair of wire-glasses that he constantly looked over on his nose. His looks and radical perspectives reminded me of H. Rap Brown, a militant icon and a civil rights movement activist who became popular in the early sixties. PO2 Ervin was very passionate about advocating Black justice, and he was not afraid to let his agenda be known all over the command.

There were several allegations concerning PO2 Ervin. Over the course of time, I had learned a number of issues about him. He was blamed to be chiefly responsible for the unrest on the base because he seemed to be defiant and would not condone any racial violations. Despite that fact, PO2 Ervin refuted all the charges against him and brought them all up to the attention of the naval commanding officer for further--hopefully unbiased--determination. After the base investigation, PO2 Ervin was recommended to be court-martialed as the final action. But PO2 Ervin did not let this alarming referral intimidate him. At the same time, most of the charges against him seemed to be murky.

Prior to the outcome of the investigation process and with the support of the Black Study Group, PO2 Ervin had written a number of letters to certain influential people outside the naval service detailing the racial friction taking place in Subic. He even referred to Subic Bay as an "institutional slavery" base for the Black sailors. His letter eventually reached The Robert Brown Elliot League, a non-profit organization in San Francisco, California advocating for racial equality. PO2 Erwin's wife called them to inform of the grievances and plight of the Black sailors in Subic, as well as the issues concerning PO2 Ervin.

Mrs. Raye G. Richardson, the present executive director of The Robert Brown Elliot

League took action on behalf of the Ervins. She reached out to Phillip Burton of California, a member of the U.S. House of Representatives, who eventually requested that the Department of the Navy in Washington, D.C. look into the situations of the Black sailors stationed in the Philippines. Based on his track record, Phillip Burton championed the welfare and civil rights of the elderly, blind, disabled, miners, immigrants, and minorities. His action resulted in a subsequent-thorough investigation alleging the unfair treatment of Blacks aboard the Subic Bay Naval Base.

During the extensive investigative procedure, it was an extremely troublesome time for the Blacks. The Naval Investigation Service (NIS) in Subic began to interrogate Black sailors about the Black Study Group, and the master-at-arms broke up a couple of our meetings because the group was suspected and perhaps feared to be subversive. The tensions among servicemen seemed to be fuming rapidly.

I was one of those who were called to report to the NIS office. Just like the others who were summoned before me, they questioned me about "the word" that they believed had come out of our meetings declaring "Get Whitey at all cost!" They were somehow concerned that the Blacks might beat up the Whites and that the Blacks might beat up the Whites and that the Blacks might start an insurrection that would undermine any lawful orders of the naval command. They also wanted to know more about the symbolic red-Afro comb that certain Black sailors carried in their left back pocket, which was viewed as a radical behavior against naval base regulations.

I knew that amid all these racial pressures and investigations, I had to protect myself, as well as my soul bothers at the boat

Barbara Perkins-Brown

I am what I am and I believe in my own nobility

The Robert Brown Elliott League
146 LEAVENWORTH STREET - SAN FRANCISCO, CALIF. 94102 Telephone: 673-7427

September 12, 1968

Hon. Phillip Burton
450 Golden Gate Ave.
Room 11152
San Francisco, California 94102

Dear Mr. Burton:

The enclosed letter is self-explanatory. We are asking for an impartial investigation of the intolerable racial at the United States Naval Station, Subic Bay, The Philippines.

Our attention was first drawn to this matter when the wife of one of the signers of the enclosed letter called us from Oakland and asked our assistance. We asked for particulars and subsequently received this letter. Yesterday, Mrs. Richardson talked via telephone to PC3 Morris G. Ervin, who has an urgent need for aid. Without any official notification, Ervin found that on September 8, 1968, he was being held for court martial--this was the date he expected to be discharged. Prior to this date he had not even been advised of the charges. We heard of his predicament too late to even ask for any direct aid for him.

Racial slurs when added to the many indignities that a serviceman has to face normally, will certainly undermine the morale of all of the personnel on any military base--black or white personnel.

Punishment for expressing grievances certainly should never be meted out to our fighting men. When, in the face of certain vengeful reaction, these young men feel so abused that they dare put in writing the enclosed entreaty for aid, certainly they should be heard and protected from this abuse.

Knowing of your past actions and your sentiments, you were, naturally, the first to come to our minds. Please do all that you can. Let us know what you think we should do.

Very gratefully,

R.B. ELLIOTT LEAGUE

(Mrs.) Raye G. Richardson
Executive Director

An independent, non-partisan political organization dedicated to ending racial discrimination

Copy of the letter sent by The Robert Brown Elliot League to Phillip Burton urging for investigation

pool so that nobody at this point could be further implicated.

"As a Navy Petty Officer, I have nothing to concur about the racial adaptability at Subic Base." Those were the only words that came out of my mouth, as my answer to all their persistent inquiries concerning all the negative commotions against Blacks that had taken place in *Subic.*

CHAPTER 5

The Accused

One week later, after I reported to NIS, I was on my boat doing my usual job as a cook. That day, I was frying chicken. I told Felipe, the houseboy that I was going to the head (restroom). I was only gone for about four minutes; however, when I returned to the kitchen, the skillet with chicken was surprisingly on fire. At the same time, I saw Chief Griffith with the fire extinguisher in his hands, struggling as if he was fighting the flame on the stove.

"What happened?" I cried out.

"Are you trying to burn down my boat? I am putting you on report!" Chief Griffith exclaimed frantically.

Immediately after the situation got under control, I tried to explain to Chief Griffith that someone must have turned up the dial on the stove while I was gone.

"You!" pointing his finger at me, "You did it, and I will get you off my boat!" accused Chief Griffith with certainty in his tone.

After the furious chief left the kitchen, I asked Houseboy what had happened while I was in the restroom. Houseboy said, in his broken English, that all he remembered was that the chief walked in and asked where the cook was, and all of a sudden, he sprayed the stove with foam.

    Two days later, after the fire incident at the boat, I was ordered to appear at the captain's mast to face the charges of duty not conforming to military supervision. The mast, under the Uniform of Code of Military Justice Article 15, was a non-judicial due process in which the commanding officer, such as the captain or admiral, would inquire into the minor offenses and charges allegedly committed by a naval member. The commanding officer would afford the offender the opportunity to explain his or her side. After the hearing, the commanding officer would render judgment such as dismissing the case, imposing punishment, or referring to a court-martial.

    After receiving the memo, I reported right away to Captain Lewis's office, the same officer who had threatened me on my first day at Subic that he "would take that crow off my arm" because I showed up late to my duty. As I walked into the captain's office, I saw Chief Griffith sitting in one of the chairs in front of the captain's desk. He did not look at me, but I noticed the sudden change in his expression from calm to resentful.

    The captain, upon seeing me, acknowledged my presence and then proceeded to inform me of my charges. Then, he plainly asked me what I had to say about the said charges. I already knew that no matter what I said, the outcome would not change. Yet, I have my faith. I had to speak up and uphold what I believed was the truth regardless whether the result would be in my favor or not. So I shared with the captain what Felipe, the houseboy, had witnessed while I was gone away from the stove. As I was revealing the facts, I could see Chief Griffith became uncomfortable in his seat. During the deliberation, I clearly expressed that the fire and the charges were possibly planned out. However, Chief Griffith immediately contradicted my words.

"I don't think PO3 Perkins is able to justify his claims. He neglected the safety regulations by burning the kitchen," the chief remarked.

It did not take that long for the captain to give his sentence; I felt that he had already made up his mind before I even got there. In support of the chief's allegations, Captain Lewis tried to reason out by asserting that all cooks had burned something at times, which made it seem I could have possibly caused the fire myself as a proof of my guilt.

"I am putting you on six-month suspension and a reduction in rate. Now, if you keep high standards and military behavior within those six months, then you can have your rate back or advancement to the next rate. That's my order! Mast is over!"

"Thank you, sir," I complied. Then I stepped out of the office to wait outside.

Meanwhile, Chief Griffith remained inside the captain's office. After a few minutes, he appeared standing in front of me. Chief Griffith's face was red, as he looked at me with his fiery eyes, and I could tell that the sight of me made his already unfavorable mood even worse.

"Get your gear off my boat and report to Boat 882!" Chief Griffith screamed, and then he walked out. From his demeaning reaction towards me, I knew then in the back of my head that the whole thing--the fire and the mast proceeding--was nothing but a frame-up against me. For what reason? I had no clue.

The following morning, I reported to Boat 882. PO1 Randy Carter, a tall White male in his mid-thirties from Arkansas, met with me and wasted no time to explain the expectations and standards on his boat. He seemed to be a nice guy, and from what I had heard so far around the boat pool, PO1 Carter had not shown any negative attitude towards the Blacks. After hearing what PO1 Carter had to say, many things came flashing to my mind, and one of them was relief. I told myself that because of all the negative things that had happened to me lately, I was more than pleased to get off Chief Griffith's boat. Somehow, I felt a sense of freedom from his disdainful control.

A couple of weeks after my transfer, PO2 Cash invited me to accompany him off base. We left late afternoon and met up with PO2 Ervin in town. Then, the three of us decided to get a couple of drinks at The Jungle area.

First, we walked around the streets and saw some Filipino friends who exchanged warm greetings with us before we went into a small bar and sat in a dim corner to have a talk. PO2 Ervin shared with us about the over-blown charges against him and those threatening letters he had been receiving with racial slurs, calling him "Nigger" and "Coon

Monkey." He said his Petty Officer in charge had taken some of the letters to the XO (Executive Officer). But to their shocking disappointment. According to the XO, the navy could not take any action against those letters. Also, such racial slurs were only dismissed as a White man's way of exercising his freedom of speech.

PO2 Ervin continued exposing what had been going on around Subic. He also mentioned to us the situation concerning Seaman Murphy Jackson, a yeoman (secretarial position) working at the administrative division, who received some threats for letting Black sailors get a copy of the newspaper *Stars and Stripes* before he would take the papers to the personnel office. The papers would come every Monday, and everyone would like to get a copy of *Stars and Stripes* to learn about the news from around the world and from back home. Aside from the sports news, which was the favorite section of many sailors, the newspaper also provided a list of Vietnam casualties from each military service branch. According to the report, Seaman Jackson was written up for disobeying a lawful order and for disrespecting a superior. He was moved from his office post as a yeoman to the boat, where he was chipping paint and painting crafts, a job that was contrary to his military training. Seaman Jackson was sentenced by the special court-martial for 60 days restriction, as well as a reduction from one pay grade (E3 to E2), and a fine of $75 a month for three months. A special court-martial was the intermediate court level with a military judge, a trial counsel, a defense counsel, and at least three military officers as members of the jury.

After a few hours of talking and drinking with PO2 Ervin and PO2 Cash, I decided to call it a night and the two agreed. Next, we all got in a jeepney cab, and PO2 Cash asked the driver to drop us off at the main gate. Finally, we parted ways to return to our individual duty post in *Subic*.

CHAPTER 6

The Team

The naval base was getting ready for the basketball season. Almost everyone was excited for the tournament that was held twice a week on Monday and Wednesday evenings. Each department entered its team in the league, and many people, civilians and military, would come to the base gym to watch and cheer for the basketball game.

I was very excited to play basketball. I joined the boat pool's basketball team because I was a sports-minded fellow and because I was young and always ready for excitement and a fun challenge. Wearing my number 9 red-jersey uniform gave me some kind of blissful relief from daily tension.

PO2 Cash was our coach. He understood the sports very well. He knew what he was doing, and he took care of his athletes. He had coached a number of years throughout his military career in the U.S. Navy and had won several basketball championships at different duty stations.

I was glad and proud to play for PO2 Cash. I was six foot two, and my position was the team's power forward. We had a great team and an exciting season. That year, we won first place, and we represented Subic Bay to play against other basketball teams on ships that came to dock at the naval base. We did not only play the teams on ships, but we also played the U.S. Air Force teams stationed in Clark Air Force Base in Angeles City, which is about an hour drive from Olongapo. Our team also competed against the teams from Manila.

Besides my personal faith that had kept my sanity, basketball became an outlet that dispelled some of my disappointments. Being able to play on the team gave me peace of mind from all the destructive attitudes and harsh penalties exercised by many high-ranking officials towards us--the Black American servicemen in *Subic.*

Bobby Earl Perkins

Number 9

Basketball Tournament

Subic Bay Gym, 1967

CHAPTER 7

The Rank

After months of waiting, the results from the navy-wide exam were finally in. I passed the examination and was eligible for advancement. The following day, I took my exam result to the personnel office to file a copy in my service folder. But the personnel officer told me that I was PNA (Passed but Not Advanced) because I appeared before the commanding officer's mast and was reprimanded on a nonconformity charge concerning the kitchen fire; therefore, I was not authorized to advance. I informed the personnel officer that the decision of the company's mast was over four months ago.

"You won't be able to advance, and that's all I intend for you to hear on the subject!" the officer insisted, and then he turned his back and walked away from the service desk.

I was left standing. I felt let down as my heart was pounding fast, and I could feel my blood was boiling inside my veins. I managed to get out of the personnel office and regained my composure even though I was highly upset. I knew for a fact that whatever information noted on my personnel record was not in compliance with the navy standards and regulations. Whoever did it and why they did it remained as a big question mark in my head.

I rushed back to my boat in disbelief. I stayed inside my room sitting on my bunk. I was still in deep thought, trying to figure out how and who could help me correct my record.

At last, I whispered a short prayer, "Lord, I don't know what to do, but You do!"

Then, I decided to write a letter requesting to see the company captain about correcting my service record. I mailed my letter, and for a few days I waited earnestly for the response. I knew it would only take three days to receive a reply from the company commander. However, two weeks had gone by, and so far, there was no answer yet from the command.

In the beginning of the third week, I went to the personnel department to verify any actions pertaining to my request. To my dismay, the personnel officer informed me that they had not seen any request or letter from me.

"That's impossible," I marveled, "it's been two weeks since I dropped the request in the mail."

"It would be better if you just send in another request chit, and then we'll see what happens," the personnel officer advised me.

I left the personnel office and went straight to see PO2 Cash. Just like many Black sailors who came to him for guidance, I needed him at this moment to help me sort out my problems. I felt like my chest was gripped by pain, and at the same time my troubled heart wanted to explode in anger. I was almost teary, and my voice was broken by hurt and rage as I told PO2 Cash everything that had been bothering me--from facing charges regarding the kitchen fire to getting a PNA stamp on my service record. Somehow, I thought the U.S. Navy had wronged me. How could they deny me of my advancement when I knew I deserved it? PO2 Cash was a good listener, and he understood my anguish.

"Have faith... Just have faith..." He gave me a gentle squeeze on my shoulder assuring me that I was strong enough to handle this matter.

PO2 Cash also suggested that I should send a letter to the area commander instead of the company captain. I agreed with his idea. I had to do what I had to do to get my own justice.

That night I drafted a letter to the area commander. I knew I had to skip the chain of command if I wanted my letter to get to the right authority.

The next morning, with the letter in my hand, I approached this Filipino sailor whom I had met before at the galley. His name was PO2 Reymond Mercado, a yeoman in the personnel office. I explained to him the subject of my letter, and without any hesitation, he assured me that he would help me and would get the letter to the right people. PO2 Mercado even typed up my letter and sent it off for me.

A few weeks later, I was summoned to the personnel office. Upon arrival, I was notified that an administrative error was found in my service record and that I would be eligible to advance my rank to Petty Officer Second Class or E5. However, I was also informed that a retroactive advancement in my case was not authorized. Before my promotion, I was required to sign a document stating that I wanted to waive my privilege to correct my service record. I had no choice but to give them my signature. I knew something fishy was going on. I could not help but wonder that whoever was behind the whole scheme to sabotage my military career could possibly be the same folks playing the same old game to discriminate the Blacks. And I knew then that I was like in a such oppressive environment--unable to confront racism that had monumentally existed in *Subic.*

CHAPTER 8

The Wound

Months had passed. I carried on my duties and did my best to adhere to military bearing in compliance with the Navy's expectations. So far everything went on as normal.

It was the weekend; almost everyone

was looking forward to it. PO2 Cash, BM Wilson, and I planned a night out. On weekends, I usually hung out with the other sailors off base for some bar hopping and light drinking as a way of unwinding from our hectic military activities. After doing my laundry, I took a shower and got myself ready for some nightlife in town. Then, I met up with the two petty officers at the main gate, and we all got into a jeepney cab, heading to The Jungle area.

  The three of us went to the Birdland Nightclub, one of our favorite hangout spots. It was getting late, but the party had just started. There were loud music, go-go dancers, cigars, and all types of alcohol for the customers' delight. Almost everyone was having a good time, including us. Later on, some fleet sailors who got off from one of the ships in port got into a fight. It was a big brawl inside the bar, and everyone was headed for the exits. It was hysterically crowded. Both customers and workers were helplessly trying to get out of the way.

PO2 Cash and I were able to get through the crowd somehow, and when we finally got outside, the Armed Forces Police (AFP) was on the streets directing the crowd to break up all the pushing and shoving. Immediately, we looked for BM Wilson among the mob. Then after a few minutes of waiting and wondering where he was, he emerged from the crowded entrance of the bar.

As soon as the three of us got reunited, we got away from the turmoil, and we started walking away from the bar. Then all of a sudden, I felt a hot flash in my body.

"You got blood on you!" PO2 Cash cried out.

Then I realized that I had been stabbed in the abdomen, and my left shoulder felt hot because it was also wounded. I felt totally weak and sore. Somehow, my brown shirt and my jeans were both covered with my own blood.

PO2 Cash and BM Wilson hurriedly called out at the AFP for help. I was not unconscious, but I could not quite recall how they rushed me back on base. The navy medical unit was standing by at the main gate waiting to take me to the hospital in Cubi Point, where I remained for three days for intensive medical care.

After my discharge from the hospital, I was ordered by the doctor to go back to work but only to perform light duties for two weeks. I was also instructed to keep my appointments at the out-patient clinic for further evaluation at the end of two weeks.

Before leaving the hospital, I received a memo to report directly to Chief Turner. When I arrived at his office, he informed me that I could go back to my old boat and that I looked good to go. I was a little confused and at the same time silently indignant. I just got out of the medical facility with 34 stitches on my aching body--12 on my shoulder and 22 on my abdomen--and the chief's decision was contrary to the doctor's medical directives. I expressed my concerns to Chief Turner that the boat was not light duty at all. However, he insisted that I got the houseboy to carry anything I could not. I tried to ask for a little consideration, but my plea fell on deaf ears. I knew inside me that this was outrageously wrong. I hated to think it this way--what could a Black man like me do about it but to obey like an old slave in a White men's world.

After about a week on the boat, with all the pulling and jerking and bumping on the ships we were docking, I felt terribly sick. I asked the chief if I could take off that afternoon to see the doctor, and he allowed me.

At the clinic, the doctor asked about the kind of work I was performing during my two-week recovery period. I told him candidly about the boat duty.

"Boat duty? You have some stitches busted! You shouldn't be on the boat," the doctor strongly emphasized, "I will call your chief!"

Because of my unexpected medical situation, I was advised to stay at the clinic that night for further observation. Even after the medication had been fully administered to me, I could still feel the oozing pain in my body. Inside a small room, as I lay there by myself, looking at the window, I prayed to God for His compassion and guidance. I simply asked Him to help me endure all the challenges in store for me while still stationed in *Subic.*

CHAPTER 9

The Mess Hall

The next morning, Chief Turner arrived at the doctor's office ten minutes after I stepped out of the small medical confinement room, where I spent the entire night. I was sitting across from him at the waiting room, and I pretended to act as if I had no clue what was going on. In my silence, I tried to analyze the chief's reactions, hopefully without him noticing me. He looked worried and guilty because he knew of his failure to obey lawful orders. He was sweating inside the air-conditioned building, and his aged face was reddish, but its expression remained sturdy and tough. In a little while, he was called inside the doctor's office while I remained quietly seated in the waiting room.

After a couple of minutes at the medical clinic, Chief Turner and I were now both heading back to his office. I was following him, and the whole time we never said anything to each other--we were like strangers. When we reached his office, only then did he communicate with me.

"You will be going to the mess hall to work the night shift as a baker," Chief Turner proceeded, "and you will be working from 1800 hours to 0300 hours. You will be working with six Filipino workers. It will be two on five off and five on two off [five days off and two days work, and then the next week, five days work and two days off]." He added, "I want you to check the workers when they finish their shift."

"Check for what?" I wondered.

"Silverware, food, and any naval items," the chief clarified.

"OK, Chief," I concurred.

Chief Turner also pointed out that I would be starting tonight. Next, he gave me a list of what to bake for the week. After ensuring that I understood his orders, he then directed me to leave.

That night, I reported to work as ordered. After meeting the people I was assigned to work with, we baked cakes and pies for the mess hall. The same night, Chief Turner came to check on us. He walked around the mess hall like he was exploring the area for the first time. Next, he checked the food we prepared in the kitchen, and then he stood up in front of me. He looked directly into my eyes with a slight crease on his lips as if he was trying to smile. He nodded his head expressing his approval and commended me by stating that I did a good job. At the same time, in the back of my mind, I was a little confused on how to define his action--was his compliment a sham or real? For me, it was hard to get motivated by someone who condoned blatant racial prejudice and deliberate injustice to the Blacks. Since I had been in this command, I heard a number of stories and even witnessed for myself the chief's disdainful treatments of Blacks. After all, being from Alabama, historically speaking, I knew certain people like him, and how these people viewed my color as inferior to them.

    When the chief left, we all went back to our designated assignment. I thought I was fine; however, there was some kind of indignation brewing inside of me as I looked back at the hardships I had gone through recently. Finally, I decided to say a prayer. Then, I consoled myself that I would not let anyone ruin my spirit, and as a "Black sailor," I would perform with pride and dignity all my duties that the naval service set forth in regulations.

On the second night, we baked doughnuts. The Filipino workers wanted to take the "doughnut holes" home. But I explained to them that the chief had ordered me that nothing should be taken out from the base mess hall. The workers insisted that they had taken home the "holes" ever since they had started working there, and it was not a big deal then. Some of them had been working on base for over twenty years, and they confirmed that the cook before me had allowed them to take home the "holes" and any leftover dough and that the former cook was White. It was a dilemma for me, but I was able to assure the workers that I would have to discuss it first with the chief before I could make a decision.

The morning came, and the first thing I did was go see Chief Turner in his office. I told him what the workers brought up to me last night concerning the "doughnut holes."

"You have your orders!" the chief reminded me and said nothing else. Then, he walked away and made himself busy by looking through some paperwork in the grey file cabinet sitting in the corner of his office.

"I will carry out my orders, Chief" I complied and acknowledged that his decision was clear and final.

Then, I left his office with a heavy thought. I felt as if the chief wanted to create a friction between me and the workers. But I was able to figure out a way around it.

The following night, I cleared up the issue with the workers. I basically notified them that whatever they got out of the dumpsters, as long as not from the mess hall, was not my business and I had no control over that. So far, I had learned that most of the other base workers would take whatever they wanted out of the dumpsters and that the base command was OK with the matter. It was a challenging situation, both mentally and morally. But then again, holding on to my deep personal conviction, I knew that I could continue to survive in **Subic.**

CHAPTER 10

The Outcry

The word of mouth circulating around the naval base was that the captain was going to be transferred to a state-side duty station. This information came after the request of a member of the U.S. House of Representatives, Phillip Burton, to call for a full-scale investigation on the discrimination issue taking place in Subic Bay Naval Base. The findings of the supposed investigation were currently under review by the Bureau of Naval Personnel in Washington, D.C.

April 4, 1968. I considered this as a dark day in American history. The charismatic civil rights leader Dr. Martin Luther King, Jr. was ruthlessly assassinated. His untimely death made a loud uproar that echoed inside Subic. The base was like a powder keg ready to blow up in flames at any second, resulting from every incident of racial abuse towards Black sailors and marines. Eventually, chaos became the norm for several days. Vengeful reactions and violent retaliations became the daily frictions inside the naval base between the Blacks and the Whites. Cars were set on fire. Buildings were trashed and burned. Some White sailors were attacked and beaten. The situations got out of order, and the navy command had no choice but to close down the military gates. No naval personnel were allowed off base for three days.

On every street, members of the military police were on guard. They were seen patrolling every building, including the mess hall, to control and maintain the peace and order. After about four days, the unsightly turmoil on base gradually toned down. However, one gruesome fact remained in Subic--the racial strife was still prevailing furtively!

The aftermath of the recent horrid activities throughout the naval base had somehow left a deep ugly scar on everyone's dignity--as a human being and as a military unit. To alleviate the stricken morale of the U.S. Navy, the base command had released a statement that Bobby Day, a famous African American rock and roll singer known for his famed-hit "Rocking Robin," would be coming to Subic's Rexall Theater for a one-night concert.

June 1968. The night of the concert finally came. Many sailors, Black and White, watched the musical performance, which was the navy's means of promoting high morale in the military and establishing racial relations among servicemen. I viewed the concert as an act of goodwill by those in authority, but humanly speaking, it was somewhat late since the damaging injury of discrimination had destroyed people, property, and peace.

Those in authority at Subic Bay had every opportunity to proactively prevent the escalation of racial tensions between the Black and White servicemen if only they chose to fairly protect everyone's constitutional rights regardless of skin color. We were all sent out to Subic to carry out an American mission, and that was to prevent a war around the Pacific; however, here we were making war among ourselves and unable to combat our own battles.

In the eyes of the foreigners and in the midst of their country, the Philippines--where Americans were aliens--we humiliated ourselves as humans and disrespected our military uniforms that supposed to serve as a symbol of U.S. pride, power, and freedom. Ironically, we seemed to be powerless and shackled by our gory past--slavery, segregation, inequality, and discrimination-- these negative experiences would continue to haunt us even away from home if we refused to heal. History could repeat itself, but only if we would allow it.

> HOUSE OF REPRESENTATIVES, U.S.
> WASHINGTON, D.C.
>
> September 23, 1968
>
> Dear Sir:
>
> The attached communication is submitted for your consideration, and to ask that the request made therein be complied with, if possible.
>
> If you will advise me of your action in this matter and have the letter returned to me with your reply, I will appreciate it.
>
> Please reply in dupl. to:
> 450 Golden Gate Avenue
> 11152 Federal Building
> San Francisco, Cal. 94102
>
> Very truly yours,
>
> PHILLIP BURTON
> M.C.
> 5th - CALIFORNIA District.

A copy of the cover letter sent to the Department of the Navy by Representative Phillip Burton of California

Although I pondered every moment how the stigma of racism was tolerated to transcend from my homeland to a foreign land, I believed that God had allowed things to happen within His will and that a lesson of "miraculous transformation" was in store for all of those who were impacted by such experience in this military facility--*Subic.*

Subic: A Sailor's Memoir

In Retrospect

September 1968. I left Subic Bay for a new duty station. PO2 Cash and I were both transferred to Point Mugu Naval Air Station in California. Even though my tour in the Philippines was somehow of a derogatory nature, from which I disconcertingly endured racism and injustice, I continued to serve in the U.S. Navy for a total of 21 years and became a Chief Petty Officer (E7) upon retirement.

I was able to withstand all those challenges in my naval career because of God's provision. I believe God sent me to the Philippines for a number of reasons, and one of those reasons was to meet a Filipina lady who became my first wife and gave me my first born child--a daughter who would later on write this memoir for me.

Subic: A Sailor's Memoir

Bobby Earl Perkins, awarded Recruiter of the Year (1975) by George Wallace, Governor of Alabama

Subic: A Sailor's Memoir

Bobby Earl Perkins, awarded Recruiter of the Year (1976) by Lambert Mims, Mayor of Mobile, AL

Bobby Earl Perkins
1979

References

U.S. Navy Rank for Enlisted

E-1   Seaman Recruit

E-2   Seaman Apprentice

E-3   Seaman

E-4   Petty Officer Third Class (PO3)

E-5   Petty Officer Second Class (PO2)

E-6   Petty Officer First Class (PO1)

E-7   Chief Petty Officer (CPO)

E-8   Senior Chief Petty Officer (SCPO)

E-9   Master Chief Petty Officer (MCPO)

MILITARY TIME TABLE

Regular Time	Military Time	Regular Time	Military Time
Midnight	0000	Noon	1200
1:00 A.M.	0100	1:00 P.M.	1300
2:00 A.M.	0200	2:00 P.M.	1400
3:00 A.M.	0300	3:00 P.M.	1500
4:00 A.M.	0400	4:00 P.M.	1600
5:00 A.M.	0500	5:00 P.M.	1700
6:00 A.M	0600	6:00 P.M.	1800
7:00 A.M.	0700	7:00 P.M.	1900
8:00 A.M.	0800	8:00 P.M.	2000
9:00 A.M.	0900	9:00 P.M.	2100
10:00 A.M.	1000	10:00 P.M.	2200
11:00 A.M.	1100	11:00 P.M.	2300

OTHER WORKS OF

Dr. Barbara Perkins-Brown, Ed.D
www.barbaraperkins-brown.com
dr.barbarabrown@yahoo.com

In the Presence of the Ultimate:
A Guide to Spiritual Inquiry

The Joys Within: Spiritual Poems and Inspirational Verses

---

54 Poems for the Lord in 2 Days

Sackcloth: Voices in Verse

Unrehearsed Lines: Love Poems (Chapbook)

Inspired by You: Teenage Memories and Love Notes
(Chapbook)

==

Dr. Barbara Perkins-Brown is an active part of Alabama State Poetry Society, Alabama Writers Conclave, Alabama Writers' Forum, Military Writers Society of America, A Galaxy of Verse, Toastmasters International, and International Society of Educational Planners.

www.ingramcontent.com/pod-product-compliance
Lightning Source LLC
Chambersburg PA
CBHW071302040426
42444CB00009B/1834